Octopus's Legs

Nicola Moon

Illustrated by Robert McPhillips

OXFORD
UNIVERSITY PRESS

Deep down in the sea there was
an old wreck.

Octopus lived in the old wreck.
Octopus had lots of legs.

One day the small fish saw Octopus.

"Octopus has lots of legs," they said.
"Let's count them."

Octopus wouldn't stay still.

The fish started to count.
"One, two, three."

Octopus danced around.

They started to count again.
"One, two, three."

Octopus danced around.

"Stay still," said the fish.
"Don't dance around."

Octopus danced around and around...

...until he got dizzy and fell to the ground!

"Now we can count his legs!"
said the small fish.

"One, two, three, four, five, six, seven..."

"Eight!"